A Celebration of Love

A Celebration of Love

Edited by Gail Harvey

Gramercy Books
New York • Avenel, New Jersey

Introduction and Compilation
Copyright © 1992 by Outlet Book Company, Inc.
All rights reserved
First published in 1992 by Gramercy Books
distributed by Outlet Book Company, Inc.,
a Random House Company,
40 Engelhard Avenue
Avenel, New Jersey 07001

Manufactured in the United States

Designed by Sara Self

Library of Congress Cataloging-in-Publication Data
A Celebration of love.
p. cm.
ISBN 0-517-08139-3
1. Underwood, Clarence F. 2. Love in art. 3. Love—Quotations,
maxims, etc. I. Gramercy Books (Firm)
ND237.U63A4 1992
759.13—dc20 92-13442 CIP

8 7 6 5 4 3 2 1

Introduction

Throughout history, lovers have provided inspiration for novelists and dramatists, poets and painters. Many have immortalized their own beloveds. Others have written of the miracle and magic of loving, while some have described the delights of being loved.

A Celebration of Love is an enchanting collection of memorable poems and prose from the pens of some of the world's great writers. William Wordsworth, for example, writes a letter brimming with love to Mary, his wife of eight years. Queen Victoria describes in her journal her joyous betrothal to her beloved Albert. John Keats writes a love letter to Fanny Brawne, although he knows he will not live to marry her. And James Joyce writes "You are my only love," in a letter to his wife, Nora.

Included, too, are wonderful poems by W.B. Yeats, Christina Rossetti, and Elizabeth Barrett Browning, as well as two of William Shakespeare's love sonnets.

With delightful paintings by the Victorian illustrator Clarence F. Underwood, this charming book pays tribute to lovers past and present.

GAIL HARVEY

New York
1992

We are human only because we love

others or have the opportunity to do so.

Boris Pasternak

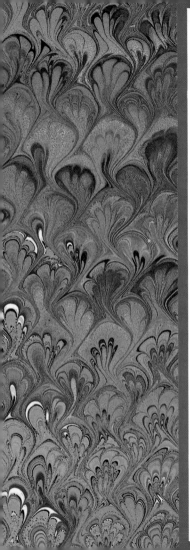

I ne'er was struck before that hour
With love so sudden and so sweet,
Her face it bloomed like a sweet flower
And stole my heart away complete.

JOHN CLARE

My love is fairer than
a summer day,
His breath it is sweeter
than newly mown hay.

OLD IRISH SONG

You are always new. The last of your

kisses was ever the sweetest; the last smile

the brightest; the last movement the

gracefullest.

John Keats, the English poet, in a
letter to Fanny Brawne whom he
met shortly before he learned that he
had tuberculosis and would never be
able to marry

Love in her sunny eyes does basking play;
Love walks the pleasant mazes of her hair;
Love does on both her lips forever stray;
And sows and reaps a thousand kisses there.

ABRAHAM COWLEY

My beloved is white and ruddy, the chiefest
among ten thousand. . . .
His mouth is most sweet: yea, he is altogether
lovely.
This is my beloved, and this is my friend.

SONG OF SOLOMON

I need your love as a touchstone of my existence. It is the sun which breathes life into me.

Juliette Drouet to her lover Victor Hugo, the French author

My heart is like a singing bird
   Whose nest is in a water'd shoot;
My heart is like an apple tree
   Whose boughs are bent with thickset fruit;
My heart is like a rainbow shell
   That paddles in halcyon sea;
My heart is gladder than all these,
   Because my love is come to me.

CHRISTINA ROSSETTI

CLARENCE F. UNDERWOOD

I love you,
Not only for what you are,
But for what I am
When I am with you.

ROY CROFT

*L*ove should run out to meet love with open arms. Indeed, the ideal story is that of two people who go into love step for step, with a fluttered consciousness, like a pair of children venturing together into a dark room. From the first moment when they see each other, with a pang of curiosity, through stage after stage of growing pleasure and embarrassment, they can read the expression of their own trouble in each other's eyes. There is here no declaration properly so called; the feeling is so plainly shared, that as soon as the man knows what it is in his own heart, he is sure of what it is in the woman's.

From Virginibus Puerisque
by Robert Louis Stevenson

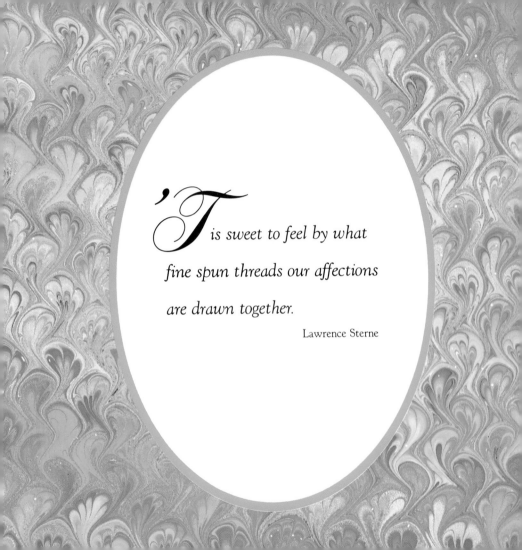

'*T*is sweet to feel by what

fine spun threads our affections

are drawn together.

Lawrence Sterne

After a youth and manhood passed half in unutterable misery and half in dreary solitude, I have had for the first time found what I can truly love—I have found *you*. You are my sympathy—my better self—my good angel—I am bound to you with a strong attachment. I think you are good, gifted, lovely: a fervent, a solemn passion is conceived in my heart; it leans to you, draws you to my center and spring of life, wraps my existence about you—and, kindling in pure, powerful flame, fuses you and me in one.

From Jane Eyre *by Charlotte Bronte*

Love is a circle that doth restless move

In the same sweet eternity of love.

ROBERT HERRICK

Drink to me, only, with thine eyes,
  And I will pledge with mine;
Or leave a kiss but in the cup,
  And I'll not look for wine.

BEN JONSON

You must believe me when I tell you that I have found it impossible to carry the heavy burden of responsibility and discharge my duties as king as I would wish to do without the help and support of the woman I love.

Edward VIII, in his radio broadcast to the people of the United Kingdom when he abdicated to marry Wallis Simpson, a commoner and a divorcée

I would rather have a crust and a tent with you than be queen of all the world.

Isabel Burton to her husband Richard, the colorful nineteenth-century explorer and writer. She shared his wanderings from the time of their marriage in 1861 until his death thirty years later, writing travel books, and his biography.

11 August 1810

*E*very day every hour every moment makes me feel more deeply how blessed we are in each other, how purely how faithfully how ardently, and how tenderly we love each other; I put this last word last because, though I am persuaded that a deep affection is not uncommon in married life, yet I am confident that a lively, gushing, thought-employing, spirit-stirring, passion of love, is very rare even among good people. . . . We have been parted my sweet Mary too long, but we have not been parted in vain, for wherever I go I am admonished how blessed, and almost peculiar a lot mine is. . . .

O Mary I love you with a passion of love which grows till I tremble to think of its strength; your children and the care which they require must fortunately steal between you and the solitude and the longings of absence—when I am moving about in travelling I am less unhappy than when stationary, but then I am at every moment, I will not say reminded of you, for you never I think are out of my mind 3 minutes together however I am engaged, but I am every moment seized with a longing wish that you might see the objects which interest me as I pass along, and not having you at my side my pleasure is so imperfect that after a short look I had rather not see the object at all.

William Wordsworth, in a letter to his wife Mary, written eight years after their marriage and shortly after the birth of their fifth child

*I*f ever two were one, than surely we.
If ever man were loved by wife, then thee;
If ever wife was happy in a man,
Compare with me ye women if you can.
I prize thy love more than whole mines of gold,
Or all the riches that the East doth hold.
My love is such that rivers cannot quench,
Nor ought but love from thee, give recompence.
Thy love is such I can no way repay,
The heavens reward thee manifold I pray.
Then while we live, in love lets so persever,
That when we live no more, we may live ever.

ANNE BRADSTREET

That is true love which always and forever remains the same, whether one grants it everything or denies it everything.

S. W. Goethe

To love someone means to see him as God intended him.

Feodor Dostoevsky

Let those

love now

who never

loved before.

Let those

who always

loved

now love

the more.

THOMAS PARNELL

You are my only love. You have me completely in your power. I know and feel that if I am to write anything fine and noble in the future I shall do so only by listening at the doors of your heart. I would like to go through life side by side with you, telling you more and more until we grew to be one being together until the hour should come for us to die.

James Joyce, the Irish writer, in a letter to Nora, his wife

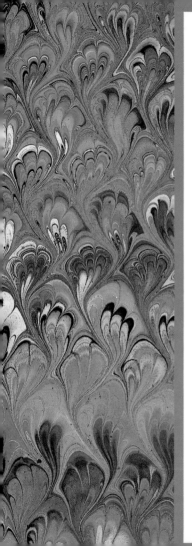

To love someone is to be the only one

to see a miracle invisible to others.

François Mauriac

To my dear husband...I give this manuscript of a work which would never have been written but for the happiness which his love has conferred on my life.

George Eliot, the English novelist, in 1859, in her dedication of "Adam Bede" to George Henry Lewes with whom she lived until his death but never married

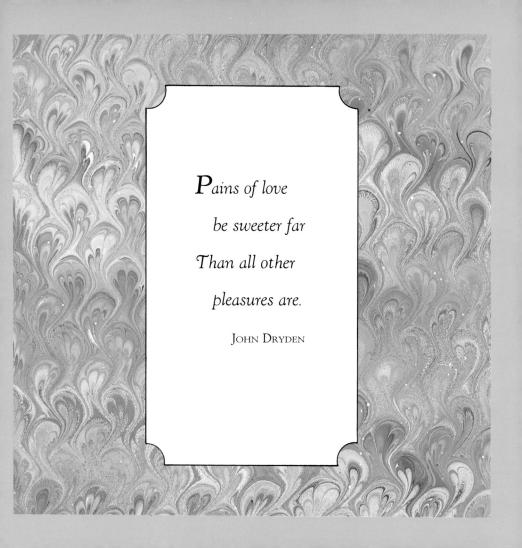

*P*ains of love

be sweeter far

Than all other

pleasures are.

JOHN DRYDEN

15 October 1839

At about ½ p. 12 I sent for Albert; he came to the Closet where I was alone, and after a few minutes I said to him, that I thought he must be aware why I wished [[him]] to come here, and that it would make me too happy if he would consent to what I wished (to marry me); we embraced each other over and over again, and he was so kind, so affectionate; Oh! to feel I was, and am, loved by such an Angel as Albert was too great delight to describe! he is perfection; perfection in every way—in beauty—in everything! I told him I was quite unworthy of him and kissed his dear hand—he said he would be very happy ⟦to share his life with her⟧ and was so kind and seemed so happy, that I really felt it was the happiest brightest moment in my life, which made up for all I had suffered and endured. Oh! how I adore and love him, I cannot say!! how I will strive to make him feel as little as possible the great sacrifice he has made; I told him it was a great sacrifice,—which he wouldn't allow...I feel the happiest of human beings.

From the Journal of Queen Victoria

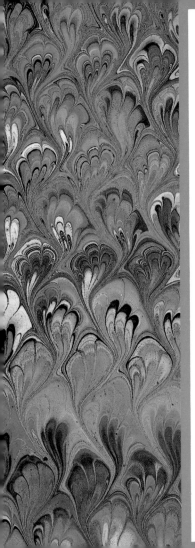

*H*ow do I love thee? Let me count the ways.
I love thee to the depth and breadth and height
My soul can reach, when feeling out of sight
For the ends of Being and ideal Grace.
I love thee to the level of every day's
Most quiet need, by sun and candle-light.
I love thee freely, as men strive for right;
I love thee purely, as they turn from praise.
I love thee with the passion put to use
In my old griefs, and with my childhood's faith.
I love thee with a love I seemed to lose
With my lost saints—I love thee with the breath,
Smiles, tears, of all my life!—and, if God choose,
I shall but love thee better after death.

ELIZABETH BARRETT BROWNING

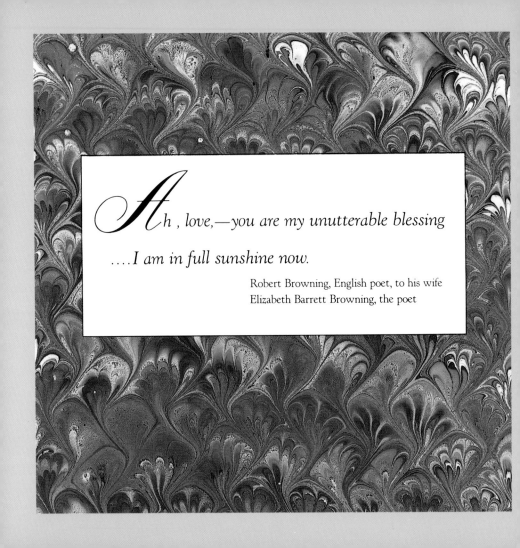

*A*h , love,—you are my unutterable blessing

....*I am in full sunshine now.*

Robert Browning, English poet, to his wife
Elizabeth Barrett Browning, the poet

I love you soulfully and bodyfully, properly and improperly, every way that a woman can be loved.

George Bernard Shaw, Irish playwright, to
Ellen Terry, the English actress with whom
he had an epistolary romance

Shall I compare thee to a summer's day?
Thou art more lovely and more temperate:
Rough winds do shake the darling buds of May,
And summer's lease hath all too short a date.
Sometime too hot the eve of heaven shines.
And often is his gold complexion dimm'd;
And every fair from fair sometime declines,
By chance or nature's changing course untrimmed.
But the eternal summer shall not fade.
Nor lose possession of that fair thou owest;
Nor shall Death brag thou wander'st in his shade,
When in eternal lines to time thou grow'st;
    So long as men can breathe, or eyes can see,
    So long lives this, and this gives life to thee.

*L*et me not to the marriage of true minds
Admit impediments. Love is not love
Which alters when it alteration finds.
Or bends with the remover to remove:
O, no! it is an ever-fixed mark,
That looks on tempests and is never shaken;
It is the star to every wandering bark,
Whose worth's unknown, although his height be taken.
Love's not Time's fool, though rosy lips and cheeks
Within his bending sickle's compass come;
Love alters not with his brief hours and weeks,
But bears it out even to the edge of doom.
    If this be error and upon me proved.
    I never writ, nor no man ever loved.

WILLIAM SHAKESPEARE

Experience teaches us that love

does not consist of two people

looking at each other, but of

looking together in the same direction.

Antoine de Saint-Exupéry

When you are old and gray and full of sleep,
And nodding by the fire, take down this book,
And slowly read, and dream of the soft look
Your eyes had once, and of their shadows deep;

How many loved your moments of glad grace,
And loved your beauty with love false or true,
But one man loved the pilgrim soul in you,
And loved the sorrows of your changing face;

And bending down beside the glowing bars,
Murmur, a little sadly, how Love fled
And paced upon the mountains overhead
And hid his face amid a crowd of stars.

W. B. YEATS

$\mathscr{T}$o love a person means to agree
to grow old with him.

Albert Camus

I love thee, I love but thee,
With a love that shall not die
Till the sun grows cold,
And the stars are old,
And the leaves of the Judgment Book unfold.

BAYNARD TAYLOR

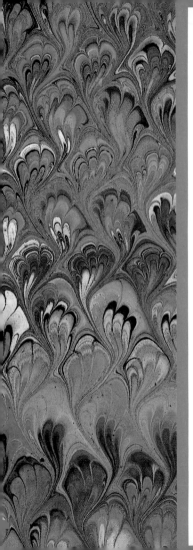

I have lived long enough to know that the evening glow of love has its own riches and splendor.

Benjamin Disraeli

I hold it true, whate'er befall,
I feel it when I sorrow most;
'Tis better to have loved and lost,
Than never to have loved at all.

ALFRED, LORD TENNYSON